ALSO BY SANDI HORTON

My House of Poetry, 2014

Cooking Without Recipes

a guide for the home cook

Copyright © 2014 by Sandi Horton

All rights reserved.

ISBN: 978-1-5007-4235-5

Cooking Without Recipes

a guide for the home cook

Sandi Horton

With gratitude for

my husband Jeff who compliments my cooking daily, encourages me to continue creating new recipes, and enjoys eating good food as much as I do!

Contents

Intro to Cooking   **11**

Shopping for Food   **19**

    Meat

    Fresh produce

    Cheese

    Bottled products

Eggs   **31**

    Scrambled, fried

    French toast, deviled eggs

    Egg sandwiches

    Omelet

    Quiche

Salads   **43**

    Garden salads and homemade dressings

    Cooked salads – chicken, potato, pasta, and bean

Chicken   **53**

    In a skillet, in an oven

Fish   **59**

    In a skillet, in an oven

    Crab cakes, salmon patties

    Shrimp, scallops

Pork   65
    Pork in a skillet, in an oven

Pasta, Rice, and More   69
    Pasta

    Sauces

    Rice, risotto

    Couscous, grits

Fresh Vegetables   77
    Asparagus, corn on the cob

    Squash

    Cauliflower, broccoli

    Cole slaw

Frozen Foods   83
    Pizza, meatballs

    Vegetables

    Breads

Mexican Style Food   91
    Quesadillas

    Chile rellenos, meat pie

    Margaritas

    Avocados, guacamole

Author Bio   99

Intro to Cooking

Intro to Cooking

It is difficult to condense decades of cooking experience into one book. Organizing cooking ideas, giving suggestions and sharing methods is an overwhelming project. I'm attempting to share my cooking discoveries to encourage others to develop their own style of cooking. It is not an easy task to limit this book to 100 pages describing the basics of creating delicious food.

Cooking is an art. It is an expression of individual taste both in food choices, combinations of different foods, and the presentation of the dishes. I like to create unique meals every day.

Recipes are too confining to me. I get exhausted just looking at all the ingredients, measurements, and instructions. Most recipes look more like a science experiment than an enjoyable cooking experience.

I like to read recipes or look at photos of food to get ideas before I create my own dish. I don't like to copy someone else's idea by following a single recipe. I usually combine several recipes or cooking ideas to invent something that appeals to my tastes. Plus, I use whatever ingredients I have on hand without any extra shopping. I feel like I'm combining art and science to produce satisfying results.

Some people seem to be natural cooks. They have an innate sense of preparing wonderful meals that taste and look good. A successful cook avoids making anything too salty or too bland, overcooked or undercooked, soggy or too hard. Timing and adding seasonings are important techniques for the serious cook.

I love eating fresh, well-prepared food. This is one reason I love cruises. There are so many excellent choices offered all day and night on a cruise ship presented in eye-appealing ways. I get most of my cooking inspiration and ideas from cruises, restaurant menus, magazines, cookbooks, and talking with other cooks.

I also get ideas for cooking by watching cooking shows on TV, reading books written by great cooks (and writers) like James Beard, Ruth Reichl, and Julia Child, by talking with my friends who love to cook, and surfing the internet. Everyone seems to have their own methods and family favorites. I learn more about cooking every day.

The two essentials things for a successful meal are:

1. A variety of fresh, quality foods that harmonize well and taste great

2. A pleasing presentation of the meal

When I start to create a meal, I first take an inventory of all my fresh ingredients and the small left-overs housed in separate containers or zip lock bags. I note which ingredients are close to losing their prime. I throw out immediately anything that has lost its texture or flavor. This hardly ever happens since I'm constantly aware of all the separate items in my refrigerator and cabinet.

I like to think about new combination possibilities. I get new ideas every time I go out to a restaurant. I love to read menus offering a variety of choices and combinations. I have a folder of restaurant menus that I sometimes read through for inspiration. I also get ideas by reading recipes in the newspaper or in magazines.

I hardly ever make a recipe that someone else has published or cooked on a TV show. I usually make changes to recipes in order to accommodate my own tastes and my own resources. Every time I cook, it is an adventure! I like to choose the selections for each meal so there is always variety.

In each meal I choose at least one food from each of these categories:

1. meat or protein: chicken, fish, pork, beef, beans, eggs
2. carbo: rice, pasta, grits, potatoes, bread, couscous

3. colorful food: vegetables, fruits, garden salads, fresh parsley, cilantro, basil leaves, celery tops

4. herbs and spices: to create a flavor of Mexican, Asian, Mediterranean, French, Italian, Indian, or American cuisines

Presentation is important to me. When creating a meal idea, I consider which serving dishes to use. I match the meal's flavors to the dishes. I use shell shaped dishes for seafood meals. Mexican food seems more festive in bold colored dishes while European food is complimented by square, elegant bistro plates or special pasta serving dishes. I use a variety of soup bowls that are different sizes, colors, and designs depending on the soup.

I enjoy finding unique dishes when I'm out shopping that match existing dishes to create new combinations of tableware/decorations. This includes small condiment serving dishes, seasonal dishes, placemats, tablecloths, cloth napkins, candle holders, etc. For my outdoor tables I have separate placemats, tablecloths, candle holders and centerpieces near the outdoor serving area.

I hardly ever use a standard dinner plate unless it's to cover something cooking in the microwave or to use as a cutting board or as a holding dish while preparing ingredients.

I also chose beverages to complement the food. For Asian meals, I serve hot tea (usually Jasmine) in a pretty teapot with matching tea cups and plates with delicate flower patterns that match the teapot. I serve Chai tea with Indian food. I serve margaritas with Mexican food, wine with European food, and iced tea with most American foods.

After choosing the best, freshest ingredients and deciding on the combinations; technique is the most important part of preparing a meal. Having the perfect flavor and texture takes practice. Everyone has their own sense of taste when it comes to herbs and spices. Some like it very spicy, some like it moderately seasoned. I use salt and pepper in almost everything. I also like sautéed onions and garlic in most entrees. I also like a little spiciness or hotness to a variety of foods, but not so much that the other flavors are overwhelmed. The trick to using herbs and spices is in knowing when to add them, then tasting to make sure it's the way you want it.

It is my hope that this book explains some basics of cooking that aren't normally found in cookbooks. Whether the reader is a beginning cook or a seasoned cook, I desire to inspire further travel on the enjoyable road to cooking unique creations.

Here are a few basics:

*Salt and pepper meat before cooking.

*Always use salt in water for rice, pasta, soup before cooking.

*Dried herbs are usually best added just before serving so they don't lose their flavor.

*Fresh herbs are best cooked with the dish. They can also be used to sprinkle on top of finished dish or set beside the food on a plate as a tasty garnish.

*Always use a small amount of spice. You can always add more, but you can't take out too much of an ingredient – especially salt.

*You can't taste too often. Taste, add, taste, add …

Technique for achieving the perfect texture in food is based on correct time and temperature. Following the time and temperature in a recipe doesn't always produce the best food. Taste, observe, and use common sense.

Once again – too little is always better than too much. You can always add extra time, but you can't undo soggy food. You can always add more temperature at the end, but you can't fix a burnt dish that was cooked at too high of a temperature or cooked too fast.

Shopping for Food

Shopping for Food

Shopping for the best quality and a variety of foods is crucial for the serious cook. This includes meat, fresh produce, spices and herbs, cupboard items, breads, and frozen foods.

Most cooking manuals and magazines suggest making weekly menus, then purchasing those items needed for the recipes. I never do this!

I do not like to feel constricted by what to cook, how to cook it and when to serve it. Therefore, I do not follow recipes exactly – recipes just give me ideas for my unique creations. I don't plan meals further than a meal or two at a time.

My mood, my schedule, the weather, and the ingredients I have 'on hand' all play a part in each meal I cook. Every morning I check my inventory of fresh produce and any stored previously cooked foods (leftovers from home or a restaurant) to decide what I want to use to make my meals. Taking a daily inventory prevents food from being wasted. Then I decide what needs to be eaten most quickly. I hardly ever throw away any food. I cook it while it's fresh.

Next, I think of pleasing combinations for those foods using different spices, sauces, pastas, rice, or cheeses. Once I have the main dish in my head, I can decide what would best compliment it in terms of variety of color, textures, and food groups. I usually serve a main dish with a vegetable, salad, and bread, plus something delicious and ornamental like fresh parsley, cilantro, sliced cucumbers, peppers, tomatoes, or fruit on the side of the plate.

Since my cooking style is one of daily creations, the most essential thing is to always have a nice selection of foods available in the refrigerator, freezer, and cabinets. This means grocery shopping is very important.

Shopping for food is an art. I keep a list on my refrigerator when I'm out of basics like eggs, butter, milk, etc. I also add any weekly grocery store specials that could help create a new dish or a favorite dinner.

First, the shopper/cook needs to know what he/she likes to eat in terms of meat, vegetables, cheeses, sauces, and seasonings. Next, the shopper must look for the freshest, best quality available.

Compare prices to discover the best foods can be the least expensive especially when it comes to fresh produce. Check for weekly sales at your grocery store.

Homemade sauces taste much better and are only a fraction of the cost. Use canned soup or broth, juice from pickle or olive jars, canned tomato products, V-8 juice, salad dressings, or sour cream. Then add your own spices.

At the end of each day, my favorite grocery store packages all meat and bakery goods at a very low price around 9-10 pm. This is a great time to shop. There are less people shopping and the grocers are sometimes restocking fresh produce for the next day so you can get first chance at the best food as well as a bargain that needs to be 'moved'.

MEAT:

Let's start with meat, the most expensive and main ingredient of my meals. I watch the grocery store ads to purchase meat when it's on sale. I package the meat into meal size portions using zip-lock bags. Then, I label it with a permanent marker before storing in the freezer. Each day I look over my meat supply to select which meat needs to eaten from the refrigerator or to select a meat from the freezer to defrost.

My freezer usually has:

chicken breasts (with bones and skin great for baking),

boneless, skinless chicken breasts (great for skillet dishes or casseroles)

chicken thighs (best for grilling)

white fish (tilapia, pangasius, catfish, etc.)

salmon (cut into serving sizes)

pork chops or end cuts

sausage (so many varieties to chose from)

bacon

previously cooked beef brisket (in meal size zip-lock bags)

previously cooked turkey brisket (in meal size zip-lock bags)

ham (sliced or chopped)

meatballs (pre-cooked)

As I look over my list of meats I notice there is hardly any beef. When I was younger I ate lots of hamburger meat in tacos, hamburgers, casseroles, spaghetti, etc. Now it is a meat I hardly ever buy except in the form of meatballs. Pre-packaged store meatballs are so easy to use. Cook according to directions then, cut each meatball into 6-8 small pieces to be used in place of hamburger meat.

We buy briskets to smoke outside and turkeys to oven roast at holidays. After the brisket is cooked and eaten for a few days, I trim all the fat before packaging the brisket into meal size zip-lock baggies to freeze for later creations. I use this same method when we cook a large turkey or ham in the oven. As soon as the dinner is over, I strip the meat from the bones, discarding all fat and skin. I divide the meat into in meal size baggies (about 1- 1½ cups of meat) before freezing. This pre-cooked meat will be used later in skillet creations or other new ways than when first served.

FRESH PRODUCE:

The second most important shopping items are fresh produce. I love looking at all the fresh foods at a grocery store, farmers' market, or roadside stands. Usually the least expensive produce is the freshest since it's most abundant when it's 'in season'.

I look forward to every spring when the fresh asparagus first comes out. Then I wait for summer when fresh corn on the cob and squash appear in huge quantities with low sale prices.

I enjoy looking at all the different kinds of squash, mushrooms, peppers, and lettuces. It is fun to try new varieties and cook them in different ways and in various combinations. Sometimes by changing or adding one ingredient in a dish, it can taste extra special and new.

I take pleasure in exploring the fresh produce aisles every time I go to the grocery store to select a variety of items. I buy whatever foods look fresh with a good price. Each shopping trip I try to buy something different from the week before. I'll decide later how to use the food in my meals. It's like being artist who is gathering lots of colors and materials.

Sometimes I have no pre-conceived ideas of the food creations I will be making. I just shop for the best food available. My mind is always churning with new ideas for a variety of entrees and sides.

Fresh carrots, potatoes, and onions, plus minced garlic in a jar are always available so I keep them in my refrigerator at all times. Carrots are a quick and easy raw snack as well as an ingredient that adds color and flavor to many dishes. Onions and garlic seem to be used every day in at least one meal at our house.

Fruits can be used many ways – as an appetizer, a side dish, a garnish on the dinner plate, or as a dessert. Most fruits in season will have a pleasant aroma and a nice texture - not too hard, not too soft and uniform color.

Peaches are a seasonal food I only buy when I can smell them as I walk by their display. Cantaloupes are fresh when the price goes down, but they are usually picked too early to have much of an aroma at the stem. Limes are biggest, juiciest and lowest priced in the spring and summer. I use fragrant limes in lots of sauces and dips as well as in my iced water, tea and mixed drinks. Cucumbers are great as a side dish instead of a salad. Cantaloupe and cucumber are also good added to iced water by the glass or pitcher.

Mangos add flavor to margaritas and add a tropical taste as a side dish to any meal. Kiwis are a pain to peel, but a slice adds such a nice color of green to the plate before serving a meal. Pineapples are also difficult to cut up, but the intense flavor is worth it. Grapes are a tasty, versatile fruit that can be used to decorate a dish, serve as a side dish, or to accompany a simple cheese platter. Different kinds of apples also go well with a variety of cheeses.

There are many choices of fruits available today. I usually buy just a few of each fruit so they don't lose their flavor and texture before I've eaten them. It only takes a couple of small pieces of a fruit to make an ordinary dish seem exotic or to be used as an appetizer.

Fruit can be added to cooked sauces or chopped to make a salsa or chutney. Be creative making combinations of fruit with different meats (especially seafood), fresh uncooked vegetables, different lettuce leaves, cheeses, sprigs of herbs, etc.

CHEESE:

The cheese aisle is another one of my favorite places to spend time in a grocery store or deli. There are so many choices, I could spend hours just trying to decide what I want each time I shop. There are over 750 varieties of cheeses from around the world. It is fun to try new kinds of cheese or to use old favorites in new ways.

I like to rotate cheeses so I don't get bored with the same flavors. Usually the store helps me decide by putting different varieties on sale. Just a touch of cheese adds so much to almost any dish whether cooked or uncooked.

Cheeses I use for cooking are grated cheeses sold in a plastic bag like Cheddar, Colby, Mozzarella, Provolone, Parmesan, Asiago, Monterey Jack, Swiss, or blends of cheeses. Chunk packages of Feta, Gorgonzola, or Bleu cheese are good to crumble up on top of a fresh green salad before serving or to add at the end of cooking meat or a sauce. Sliced cheeses can be used in sandwiches or melted on top of food creations. I serve fresh deli cheeses with olives and bread as an appetizer or as a dessert with fruit. Some of my favorites are Gouda, Havarti, Edam, Brie, Camembert, Emmentaler, and Manchego.

PREPARED BROTHS/SOUPS/ DRESSINGS:

Shopping for different liquids to use in cooking can be fun. There are so many choices! I can spend hours searching the rows of different products available. I'm always looking for new things to try to add a unique taste to my creations. Recently I discovered a Thai curry coconut broth. It is great for cooking fish, to use instead of water for making rice, or to add to stir fry vegetables. Canned fat free chicken broth helps keep dishes healthy and flavorful.

Canned cream of mushroom soup has many uses besides to eat as soup. It can be used to pour over meatballs, in green bean or other casseroles, to sauté or bake chicken, etc. Other cream soups such as cream of celery, cream of chicken, or cream of asparagus can add flavor to many newly created dishes.

Bottled salad dressings can also be used for cooking. They are much less expensive than most prepared sauces and have mostly the same ingredients. Some of my favorites are Asian Ginger Sesame dressing (great to cook pork, fish or chicken), Caesar Dressing (wonderful in pasta salads or cooked sauces), and Ranch Dressing (can be used with almost anything!).

Once again, there are so many choices on the shelves today. It is fun trying to decide how to use the different dressings in different dishes. Read the labels to find out exactly what is in each dressing. Sometimes I get cooking ideas just by reading labels. There may be a combination of ingredients I hadn't thought to put together or hadn't used in a long time.

Hot sauces come in more varieties than just the old fashioned picante sauce. Many different kinds of peppers and other ingredients are used. Some even have fruit added for an interesting twist. These sauces can be used in cooking meats or vegetables or served on the side as a relish/condiment.

Don't forget to keep traditional sauces on hand to add to your cooking creations like Worcestershire sauce, Hoisin sauce, balsamic vinegar, soy sauce, and spicy mustard.

Eggs

Eggs

This morning after eating omelets for breakfast, my husband told me, "I'm not going to hound you, but the world would be a better place if you wrote your cookbook." My 20-something year old daughter has also asked me several times, "When are you going to finish your cookbook? I need it!"

Eggs are one of the most versatile, healthy, and inexpensive food items that are readily available at any grocery store. Eggs are tasty for breakfast, lunch, or dinner and rarely take much preparation time. Eggs are quick, easy, and nutritious.

Here are some egg basics. Always use a nonstick pan and plastic utensils when making eggs. Metal utensils will damage nonstick pans. Cook all eggs on the stove's 'medium' setting -- never higher. Good egg dishes cannot be rushed or they will not have a nice texture. Raw or rubbery eggs are not appetizing.

When my daughter was a preteen with several friends spending the night, her younger brother wanted to cook breakfast for the girls. He was taking orders for pancakes and eggs. One girl told him she wanted eggs and he asked, "How do you want your eggs cooked?" She replied, "What do you mean? I just want eggs." Then he asked, "Do you want them scrambled or fried?" She answered, "I don't know. I just want eggs. That's what we have at my house." He proceeded to explain different ways to cook eggs to find out what she called 'just eggs'. This was an eye opening experience. I was amazed at the lack of culinary knowledge of average kids.

Scrambled eggs: Break eggs into a bowl. Whip with a fork until the yellows and whites are all one color and smooth. Add one tablespoon of water for each egg in the bowl. Whip again. Add salt, pepper, and any other spice you want. Add oil to skillet. Heat on medium. Pour in eggs. Wait a few minutes before stirring with a plastic spoon.

Variations: Add some spicy or Dijon mustard to eggs when beating them. While cooking, add fresh ingredients that have already been sautéed such as onions, peppers, mushrooms, garlic, etc. Just before serving add a seasoning such as basil, parsley, cumin, or oregano. Fresh chopped tomatoes can also be added when cooking or served on top of cooked eggs. Don't add too many choices or the flavors get lost. Decide which flavors you like in combination. Make hot sauce available to add after serving. There is quite a variety of red and green sauces such as picante, habanero, and tomatillo, on the market. Some sauces even have fruit flavors like raspberry, apricot, watermelon, or pineapple added that add a touch of sweet flavor to the spicy taste.

Fried eggs: Pour bacon grease or cooking oil (about 1 t. per egg) into bottom of the nonstick skillet. Use medium heat. Crack eggs into skillet. Cook until desired doneness. For sunny side up, do not flip. For regular fried eggs, flip over when they are beginning to 'set' and are no longer runny. For a dry center (good for sandwiches) gently break egg yolk at the beginning of cooking or when turning the egg.

French toast: Heat a nonstick skillet or griddle on medium heat. Whip an egg or two just like you would for scrambled eggs, but don't add water. Add some milk and whip with a fork. Cinnamon can be added. Lay bread of choice in the mixture coating both sides. Melt butter or use oil in the skillet. Place bread in oiled skillet. Cook until golden brown then, flip over. The second side takes much less time than the first side.

Egg Sandwiches

One of my favorite sandwiches is the fried egg sandwich. It's a quick and easy hot sandwich. While the egg is cooking, spread lots of mayo on the bread. Add fresh spinach leaves, arugula, thin cucumber slices, or spring mix salad leaves and you have a great sandwich. Bacon and fresh parsley chopped together make a nice combo on an egg sandwich. Any left-over meat (ham, chicken, pork chop) can be heated and added to an egg sandwich. Fresh, cooked asparagus is also a great addition.

Use the best bread available for the best sandwiches. Some of my favorites are: multigrain with walnuts or hazelnuts, dark rye or pumpernickel, 100% whole wheat, 12 grain, or poppy seed bread. Toasted English muffins also make a great egg sandwich. Melt cheese on top of the fried egg in a toaster oven. Garnish with cilantro, parsley, or fresh basil.

There are so many choices of breads today. I buy a different one each week and can go a month or longer without ever repeating a bread. This makes toast or sandwiches much more tasty and adventuresome. Before serving, always cut sandwich/toast in half for ease of eating or spreading butter and jam.

The choice of jams is also fun to select. I like to have several varieties on hand. Meals are more enjoyable when there is a new flavor or combination. Routine meals can be boring. Jams can also be added to cooking sauces for meat especially pork or fish.

Boiled eggs/deviled eggs: Place eggs in a saucepan. Cover with water. Bring water to a boil on high. Then turn down to low or whatever setting is needed for the water to continue to slightly bubble. Set timer for 5 min. Check for doneness by lifting an egg out of the water in a large spoon. If the surface dries quickly, it is done. If it remains wet a long time, cook a few more minutes. After cooking, drain the eggs and place in cold water.

To make deviled eggs: Peel the boiled eggs. Cut eggs in half. Remove the yellow balls (egg yolk) from the center. Place yellows in a bowl. Stir in your choice or combination of mayo, mustard, spicy mustard, sour cream. Add salt, pepper, curry, parsley, or any seasoning. Add pickle relish, finely chopped pickles, olives or anything else you wish. Blend well. Place mixture back in the white cooked egg half. Sprinkle with paprika. Only choose a few ingredients to add to your egg yolk or you won't be able to taste the flavors.

Omelets: Whip up eggs just like scrambled eggs using 1 tablespoon water per egg. Add salt and pepper. Pour into skillet greased with a good olive oil. Add cheese and other ingredients. Cook on medium heat until the edges are dry and it is no longer runny. Be patient. Good omelets take time. Fold omelet in half when almost done. Cook a few more minutes. You may flip it if you wish to reheat the other side.

Omelet Variations: Sautéed onions and/or mushrooms are good in all omelets!

Italian: I add Dijon or spicy mustard (about a teaspoon for 2 eggs) to my eggs before cooking. It takes a while to beat it in, but is worth the extra flavor. Add Italian seasonings (oregano, basil, parsley) or a store blend. Chopped olives, prosciutto, or sausage are also good to add. Then use a blend of Italian cheeses: Mozzarella, Provolone, Asiago, Fontina, Romano, and/or fresh Parmesan.

Greek: Use Feta cheese and Greek seasoning. Chopped or halved kalamata olives are also good.

Ham: Add left-over pieces of ham cut-up. Use Swiss, Havarti, or Cheddar cheese. This is also good with Dijon or spicy mustard mixed in the eggs.

Steak, pork, sausage: Add diced pieces of left-over meat. Sometimes I trim my steak or pork chops *before* serving. (Otherwise, I would eat all the meat at my meal.) I place the cut up pieces of meat in a zip-lock bag for my eggs or another dish I'll create the next day.

Skillet Egg Combinations

For a crowd or just as a variation, cook all ingredients usually used in an omelet in a skillet. Start with the longest cooking ingredient like onions if you don't have some already precooked in an airtight container in your refrigerator. Sauté in a good olive oil, then add more fresh items like celery, peppers, mushrooms, jalapenos. This is a good chance to clean out your refrigerator with little odds and ends of tastes. Almost anything goes well with eggs.

Be creative. Make a new combination every time you make eggs. Add some precooked breakfast meat like sausage, bacon, ham, or your zip-lock bag of meat from a previous meal. Add seasonings just before serving like basil, oregano, or chopped fresh tomatoes. Fresh parsley or cilantro always goes well on any egg dish. Mexican hot sauce or sour cream is also a great accompaniment to egg dishes.

Fresh sauces for egg dishes:

Pico de Gallo – finely chopped tomatoes, onions, and cilantro leaves (discard stems)

Red pepper sauce – use a blender or food processor to puree tomatoes, red bell peppers, and garlic with a little olive oil and salt.

Quiche:

With the convenience of premade pie shells, either frozen or refrigerated, making a quiche is one of the quickest and easiest entrées I can think of. First, beat eggs with a fork just like making scrambled eggs. Then, add other ingredients.

The basic quiche recipe is 3 eggs, 1 C. milk, 1 C. grated cheese, and 1/2 t. salt.

The variations are endless. Any kind of grated cheese or combination of cheeses can be used. (Making a quiche can be a good way to clean out your cheese drawer.)

Add other ingredients to the cheese. Fresh or frozen vegetables like spinach or broccoli are popular choices. Bacon or ham can be added to any combination in a quiche. Sometimes I add sautéed onion, garlic, celery and/or mushrooms.

Spices are a personal choice. Italian seasonings and pepper blend with almost any combination. I've even used cinnamon, nutmeg and/or cloves with ham or bacon for a unique taste. When you make your quiche, check for ingredients in your refrigerator that need to be used. It only takes a small amount of each ingredient.

Once again, don't use too many different items or you'll lose the individual flavors. Think of flavor combinations you've previously eaten or seen on a restaurant menu, then pick the combination that fits your palate that day. Next check your spice supply to discover the flavors you are in the mood to use with the combination you have chosen.

After mixing all your ingredients, pour into pie shell. Bake in preheated oven or toaster oven at 450 degrees for 15 minutes, then turn to 350 degrees for 30-40 more minutes depending on how many and what kind of ingredients you used and your oven's variance in temperature. A knife inserted in the middle will reveal if your quiche is done or not. If the knife blade is clean, the quiche is done. If there is gooey egg on the knife, keep cooking it. Recheck every 5 minutes.

Any kind of garden salad or fresh fruit can accompany a quiche.

Salads

garden, chicken, potato, pasta, and bean

Salads

When the weather gets warm, it's time for salads. Garden salad, chicken salad, pasta salad, potato salad, bean salad… The choices are unlimited!

Garden Salads:

Garden salads can be used to accompany a meal or can be large enough to serve as an entrée. The combination of ingredients is endless. When I grocery shop, I look for the freshest, best priced salad ingredients starting with lettuce, spinach, arugula, or a pre-mix of spring greens.

Salad in a bag is usually more expensive and a smaller quantity. The bags of salad are good to take to work to keep in an employee refrigerator. You can just shake out how much you want to go with your lunch each day with a minimum of effort and add a bottled dressing.

For an 'at home' meal, I prefer to make a freshly made, unique salad with a variety of ingredients with a homemade dressing. I usually mix iceberg, Romaine, or leaf lettuce with spring mix greens (usually includes arugula, radicchio, endive, watercress or others).

Individually wash each leaf of lettuce, discarding any leaves that are discolored or limp. Tear off and discard thick or spiny white parts of the lettuce. Shake out excess water before drying on top of paper towels. Gently blot to dry the top of the leaves with soft napkins. While the lettuce continues to air dry, assemble and prepare other ingredients.

Fresh chopped celery, garden or purple onion, different colored bell peppers, squash, cucumbers, radishes, carrots, nuts, dried cranberries, avocado, strawberries, mango are just a few choices for a garden salad. Crumbled cheese like gorgonzola, feta, bleu or hard grated cheese like parmesan can also be added. Offer fresh ground pepper when serving.

<u>Homemade dressings:</u>

Our favorite dressing is light olive oil with raspberry or balsamic vinegar. Herb infused oil can also be used. I especially like basil oil. Drizzle the salad with the olive oil first. Don't drown it. Splash on the vinegar. Then toss gently to disperse flavors.

Ranch dressing can be made by combining equal amounts of milk, sour cream, and mayonnaise. Add a splash of vinegar, any kind. Some fresh squeezed lime juice adds a nice flavor. Add fresh ground pepper. Fresh herbs such as chives or parsley or other spices may be added.

Honey-Mustard dressing can be made using equal parts of honey and Dijon mustard. Add white wine or cider vinegar until desired consistency and flavor. Add salt and pepper to taste. Other spices or fresh lime juice can also be added.

COOKED SALADS - Chicken, Potato, Pasta, and Bean

One of our favorite salad entrees is chicken salad. This same recipe idea can be used for pasta salad or potato salad. Just use potatoes or pasta in place of the chicken.

Basic recipe: chicken (potato or pasta) + fresh produce + canned or bottled ingredients + spices + creamy liquid mixture

Leftover grilled chicken is especially good to use. Store-bought rotisserie chicken leftover pieces also work great. Just chop up any cooked chicken.

Place chicken in a mixing bowl and start adding ingredients. First add some fresh cut up produce like celery, apples, bell pepper, onion, or whatever you like. Then add cut up prepared foods like pickles, nuts, (pecans, pine nuts, walnuts, whatever), olives, dried cranberries, etc. Don't use too many different foods or the tastes will clash. Pick out a couple of food item combinations that appeal to you when you are making the salad.

Each time you make a chicken salad it will be different depending on what you have on hand that day and what you feel like eating. Now you're ready for the liquid mixing ingredients.

Creamy liquid mixture:

Use a small bowl to stir together mayonnaise with a little mustard (Dijon, spicy, deli, or regular), sour cream, ranch dressing or any salad dressing (be creative, but don't use too many different liquids at once) Then chose a spice or spice combination - basil, curry, parsley, oregano, rosemary or a blended spice like Mrs. Dash or Creole seasoning, etc. Always read the ingredients on the spice jar. Lemon pepper is usually mostly salt. You won't need to add as much salt if your spice contains salt. Lastly add salt and pepper. Blend until creamy. Taste. Stir into chicken mixture.

Make this salad hours or a day before serving time so the flavors can mingle. Always taste your creation before storing and again before serving.

For Potato Salad: You can leave skins on or not whatever is your preference. Cube the raw potato. Place in saucepan. Cover with water. Add salt. Boil. Reduce heat to simmer. Put on a lid. Cook until potatoes cannot be picked up with a fork. Drain in a colander. Start adding ingredients. Add fresh produce like celery or onion. Then mix your choice of liquid ingredients and spices in a bowl before adding to potatoes. Dried rosemary is one of our favorite spices.

For Pasta salad: chose your favorite pasta - there are so many to choose from. (rigatoni, elbow, shell, bow tie) I love shopping for pasta buying different ones each time I go to the grocery store and keeping several choices on hand to go with my tastes and ingredient choices the day I'm cooking pasta.

Cook according to directions on the package -- each kind of pasta has a different length of cook time. DON'T overcook-taste it before time is up. Re-taste until pasta is the texture you like. Drain in colander. You may want to use an olive oil and/or balsamic vinegar in this salad as the main liquid or you may want a creamy mayo kind of macaroni salad.

Add cut up fresh produce such as celery, bell peppers, tomatoes, squash, cucumbers, basil, etc. Add canned products such as pine nuts, olives, pickles, etc.

Start by pouring bottled salad dressing (Caesar, ranch, thousand island) into a bowl. Add to taste some of the following: sour cream, mayo, mustard (Dijon, spicy, deli), or balsamic vinegar with spices like Italian seasoning, curry, parsley. Mix together. Add liquid ingredients to pasta/fresh ingredients.

Store salad in an air-tight container. Serve on torn up lettuce or spring salad mix from a bag.

It's amazing to notice the similarities among three such different salads. All food preparation uses the same basic formulas.

Main ingredient (pasta, potato, bean, or chicken) + fresh produce + canned or bottled products + spices

For a hot pasta salad: Use a skillet to sauté onions in olive oil. After about 10 minutes add choice of garlic, celery, or bell peppers to onions and continue to cook about 3-4 min. Add any fresh veggies you like that has been cooked slightly in the microwave after it has been cut down to bite-size. I especially like sliced squash, eggplant, or frozen vegetable medleys. (Lay veggies on a plate. Sprinkle with water. Cover with a paper towel. Microwave about 1 min. depending on thickness. Don't cook completely.)

Add cooked pasta to sautéed cooked veggies. Sprinkle with seasonings. Add some fresh tomato pieces, olives, pine nuts, or whatever you have that sounds good. Sprinkle with Italian type seasoning and cheese before serving.

For Black Bean/Sausage Salad:

Choose a can of beans (black, kidney, black-eyed peas, or left-over beans cooked from their dried form), optional can of corn or hominy. Drain in colander. Shopping for beans is also fun since there is such a variety on the market. Keep several varieties on hand. Experiment with different beans so you can decide what flavors you want to add to which kind of bean. Dried beans are great to make when feeding a large crowd and you have extra time. They are inexpensive and taste better than canned beans. Just follow the package directions.

Most packaged turkey, polish or kielbasa sausage is ready to eat without cooking. It can be cut up and added to the bean salad.

Chop fresh celery, onions, bell pepper, tomatoes, avocado, or cilantro. Add to colander. Canned olive slices, corn, hominy, or jalapenos can also be added.

In a large bowl mix some oil with spices (Cajun, chili powder, cumin, coriander, lemon pepper, etc.) Add salt and pepper as needed along with fresh lemon or lime juice. Add colander ingredients to mixing bowl.

Bean salad can be stored in an air tight container in the refrigerator for hours or days. Serve as a main dish, side dish, or as a dip with tortilla chips.

Chicken

Chicken

CHICKEN BREASTS

Chicken breasts are best baked or cooked in a skillet on top of the stove with a lid. Both methods are similar. First season the chicken with fresh ground pepper and salt. Then heat a small amount of olive oil in a skillet over medium heat to quickly brown the chicken skin. This will make the breast look nice and seal in the moisture. It will look done, but of course, it will still be raw on the inside.

Next, choose a liquid to cook the chicken in. The choices are unlimited – choose whatever you have on hand that your tastes buds are hungry for. Popular choices are: undiluted canned soups like tomato, cream of mushroom, cream of chicken, cream of celery, can tomatoes with green chilies, leftover white wine straight from the bottle, or a salad dressing like Sesame Asian, Vidalia onion, Thousand Island, etc.

For stove top cooking, place small amount of liquid in skillet or stockpot. Dilute with wine or water. Place chicken on top of liquid. Bring to a boil, reduce heat to very low to simmer. Put on the lid.

Onion slices, celery, and seasonings may be added before cooking. Cook until meat is done. Check by slicing thickest part with a knife to see if meat is cooked thoroughly. Depending on the size and thickness of the meat, it could take anywhere from 20 minutes to 45 minutes.

For oven roasting, place chicken in about 2 inches of water to make a rich broth for gravy or soup. Place lid on pan/baking dish or cover with foil if you don't have a lid. Sometimes I use a glass pie plate with foil. If you don't need a rich broth, don't use water. Instead, place liquid soup or dressing on top of chicken before baking. A slice of onion directly on the chicken and under the soup added lots of flavor.

Sometimes I don't use any liquid or a lid, just sprinkle parmesan or Romano cheese on top of chicken and bake until done. It usually takes 40 min. to an hour at 350 degrees depending on the size of the pieces. It can also be cooked in a toaster oven.

DRESSING/STUFFING

Make a recipe of cornbread. I prefer stone ground cornmeal for the richest flavor. I also use melted margarine instead of oil. While the cornbread is cooking, sauté chopped onion in oil in the skillet used to brown the chicken, and then add celery the last few minutes of cooking. Season veggies well with poultry seasoning or sage, fresh ground pepper and salt while mixture sits in the skillet while cooling. Chopped pecans make a nice addition. Mushrooms sautéed in butter can also be added. Be sure to salt the mushrooms when cooking to pop out their flavor.

When cornbread is done, crumble it into a large bowl, and then add the onion/celery/spice mixture and some canned chicken broth. Stir. Taste. Re-adjust seasonings. Bake for about 30 minutes at 350 degrees.

Left-over cooked chicken

I usually cook extra chicken breasts to use for completely different meals later in the week.

Chicken is especially good added to pasta whether it's frozen cheese tortellini or ravioli or freshly cooked pasta with a sauce.

Cooked rice, canned cream soup + some milk, and cubed chicken make a great casserole. Add seasoning of your choice. Then add grated cheese on top. Bake until done.

Chicken is great in an Asian stir-fry. Heat skillet with olive or peanut oil, then add some veggies:

<u>fresh</u> (mushroom, onion, celery, eggplant, or peppers),
<u>canned</u> (water chestnuts, bean sprouts)
<u>frozen</u> (broccoli, snow peas, carrots).

Season the stir-fry with ginger, curry, soy sauce, Hoisin sauce, black bean sauce, sesame Asian salad dressing or a combination. Chunky peanut butter or almond slivers can also be used. Serve on rice or ramen noodles.

Fish

Fish

FISH IN A SKILLET

Cooking fish in a skillet is easy, quick, tasty, and healthy.

I always have fish in my freezer. My favorite fish are salmon, pangasius, and tilapia. Fish thaws faster than most other meats or can be hastened by using the defrost setting on the microwave for a minute or two.

Use a nonstick skillet on medium heat.

Add enough liquid to barely cover the bottom on the skillet. No oil or butter is necessary. Pick one choice to use as liquid depending on your taste buds the day you are making the fish: seasoned or unseasoned broth; salad dressing such as Asian Sesame, Thousand Island, or Vidalia onion; any canned cream soup; any kind of hot sauce such as picante, habanera, tomatillo; juice from a jar of dill pickles; or left-over wine. Be creative. The variations are endless.

Start heating the liquid while you season your fish. Season the raw fish on both sides with at least salt and pepper. Many times I use lemon pepper which is mostly salt (always read the ingredients before using a spice blend to see if it has salt).

Place fish in a skillet, cook 4-8 minutes on each side depending how thick the fish is. The sauce will increase in volume rather than decrease as it is cooked. Juice and seasoning from the fish will create a rich sauce.

Serve fish with rice or pasta. Fresh parsley or cilantro can be served on the side. Fresh dill or basil on top of the cooked fish make it tasty and attractive.

FISH IN AN OVEN

If you are using the oven to heat bread or for a side dish or dessert, cook the fish at the same time. A good temperature for cooking just about anything is 350 degrees.

Place foil in a baking dish. The foil makes clean-up easily. Sprinkle seasoning on the fish. Spread a spoonful of thick dressing or soup on top of each fillet. Cook 8-12 minutes depending on your oven and the size of the fish fillets. You can turn the fish over halfway through the cooking if you want, but it isn't necessary.

FISH IN A FOIL POUCH

Chop onions, celery, olives, peppers, veggies (slightly cooked), pecans, or whatever you feel like. Place each fish fillet on a piece of foil. Add your choice of seasoning and chopped items, plus a teaspoon of liquid or butter to season the veggies. Wrap tightly. Place foil pouches in baking dish or pan. Cook about 15-20 minutes. This is great served with a side of buttered rice. Frozen vegetables and a seasoning like curry, saffron, basil, oregano, etc can be added to the rice before serving.

CRAB CAKES OR SALMON PATTIES

Canned crab or salmon can be used for a tasty, easy, last minute meal.

Drain the meat before adding salt and pepper or lemon pepper. In a bowl add whatever ingredients you like. I usually use a squirt or two of spicy or Dijon mustard, sautéed onions and garlic, and then something crunchy like celery or crushed up crackers or flax seed tortilla chips. I always seem to have a few fancy crackers left over from a previous appetizer offering.

Additional seasonings can be added to give the meat a Cajun (spicy) flavor or Italian (parsley, oregano or a blend) flavor. Additional ingredients like salad dressings or lime can create a unique creation.

After seasoning the meat, shape into small patties the size of your palm. Cook in heated olive oil in a skillet at the medium setting until done.

Serve with something green (garden salad, Cole slaw, fresh/frozen vegetable) and something white (pasta, rice, couscous, hot bread with butter, bread with olive oil dipping sauce)

SHRIMP AND SCALLOPS

Start by sautéing onions and garlic in olive oil. Add fresh shrimp (peeled) and/or bay scallops with salt, pepper, and any other seasonings you want. Cook 4-5 minutes then, check for doneness. Do NOT overcook. Add an Alfredo sauce (from a jar). Heat. Pour over cooked pasta. Top with green onion tops or fresh basil.

Shrimp is also great boiled in a large pot of boiling water for 5 minutes. The shrimp will turn pinkish when it is done. Serve boiled shrimp unshelled. It's fun to peel and eat with friends. Serve shrimp hot with individual dipping dishes filled with melted butter or serve cold on ice with individual dipping dishes of a red seafood sauce. You can make the red sauce by blending catsup, horseradish, and lemon juice. Worcestershire sauce or tarragon can be added for extra flavor.

Pork

Pork

PORK:

Pork comes packaged in the meat counter in several ways – pork chops, pork loin, end cuts, butterfly, etc. Boneless cuts are much easier to use especially in casseroles. The two most common ways to cook pork is in a skillet or in an oven. There are hundreds of variations using these two basic methods.

Pork in a skillet

Salt and pepper both sides of each piece of meat. Additional seasonings can be added at the discretion of the cook. Some spices that go well with pork are coriander, oregano, rosemary, ginger, or curry.

Add about ½ to 1 teaspoon of a sauce to each side of the pork. Rub sauce into the salt and pepper on the raw meat before cooking. Some of my favorite sauces to use are Asian black bean sauce, mango chutney, orange marmalade, plum jam, spicy mustard, BBQ sauce, or balsamic vinegar. Just like fish, the meat will get juicer as it cooks making more of its own sauce. (Do NOT add oil or flour.)

Cook in nonstick skillet using medium heat until both sides are done. The thicker, larger pieces take longer to cook. There should be no pink in the center of the pork when it is done.

Instead of a sauce, the meat can also be cooked in any liquid poured in the skillet before cooking. I like to use orange, pineapple or cranberry juice. Canned broth or wine can also be used.

If you're making cole slaw with some canned pineapple, use the juice from the pineapple to cook the pork.

Pork in an oven:

Line a baking dish with foil for easy clean up. Salt and pepper both sides of meat. Place pork in a single layer on the foil. Each piece can be topped with a thin slice of onion before adding soup or sauce. Use about a tablespoon of undiluted tomato or mushroom soup on top of each piece of meat. Other spices can be added to the soup before cooking. Fresh herbs like basil, chives, cilantro, or parsley can be added on top of the meat after cooking or served on the side.

Mushrooms sautéed in salted butter can be added to pork cooked in a skillet or the oven just before serving.

Pasta, Rice, and More

Pasta, Rice, and More

Pasta:

I love to keep a variety of pastas on hand so I can select the pasta I want to use with ingredients I have on hand. Some of my favorites are bow tie, macaroni shells, rigatoni, linguini, spaghetti, ziti, tortellini, bow tie, and egg noodles. I also like to have whole wheat and regular pasta. The whole wheat pairs better with beef or pork while the regular pasta usually goes better with chicken, fish, or a white sauce. It looks nice to store the different pastas in glass jars on the counter top.

When cooking the pasta always bring water to a rolling boil with salt added before adding pasta. I like to break up my spaghetti into 2 or 3 pieces before cooking to make it easier to eat. Set timer to minimum suggested time. Check for done when the timer goes off. There is nothing worse than soggy pasta. It should be firm, but not chewy. Drain in a colander.

I like to drizzle the cooked pasta with extra virgin olive oil and toss the pasta before adding the sauce or meat. This adds extra richness. Fresh basil leaves or chopped chives just before serving add flavor to any sauce.

Sauces:

Sauté fresh mushrooms and garlic in soft margarine, then add chicken and/or chopped olives. To make a sauce add some sour cream and a bit of salad dressing like Vidalia onion or Caesar. Stir in fresh ground pepper, salt, and a spice like oregano. Then heat on low. Heat up left-over pasta (or make fresh pasta). Add to sauce. Serve with fresh basil leaves on top or fresh parsley on the side. Diced fresh tomatoes can be added on top of a white sauce.

Red marinara sauces in a glass bottle are easy to heat and are inexpensive. Adding freshly sautéed mushrooms, garlic, onions, peppers, celery, or left-over red wine to the bottled sauce can make it taste almost homemade.

Canned cream of mushroom or celery soups can also be used for a quick meal. Remember to always add something fresh to canned products. Just adding fresh basil on top or parsley on the side elevates the meal from ordinary to elegant. Other side decorations could be fresh sliced tomato, cucumber or different colored bell peppers.

Frozen broccoli or peas goes well with most pasta or rice. Just add broccoli to the boiling water the last 5-6 minutes of the pasta cooking time. Drain. Toss with butter instead of oil. Other frozen vegetables or leftover vegetables from your refrigerator can be also be added.

Of course, a fresh garden salad and bread always complements pasta. Bread can be heated in the oven with garlic and butter or served with extra virgin olive oil in a dipping dish. Add a dash of balsamic vinegar or some dried rosemary for extra flavor.

Rice or Risotto Variations:

Rice and risotto are easy to make, but require the cook to pay attention.

Always check directions on the package before you start. Usually, mix 2 parts water or broth to 1 part rice. Some risottos or brown rice require more water. Always add 1 t. salt per cup of rice if using water. If using broth, check the ingredients to see if salt has already been added. It is impossible to add the salt flavor after the rice has cooked. Boil water. The pot will boil over if the cook is distracted. Add rice and salt. Cover. Turn heat to simmer. Set timer for 15 min. for most rice. Brown rice or risotto will take much longer (45 minutes - 1 hour)

Cheese rice:

Chunks of cheese can be added while the rice is cooking. Stir after cheese starts to melt. One night when making risotto to accompany a beef dish, I added cubes of pepper jack cheese. It was wonderful.

Rice with Veggies:

My favorite rice dish is plain cooked white rice (always add salt BEFORE cooking) topped with fresh cooked asparagus. I like lots of soft margarine added on top.

Sometimes I add some frozen vegetables during the last 5 minutes of cooking the rice. One night I'll add some chopped broccoli or peas, another night I'll add a medley of veggies. When using leftover cooked vegetables, add about one minute before serving to heat up the vegetables. Mushrooms, celery, onions, red, green, or yellow peppers can also provide an interesting variation.

Rice seasonings:

No seasoning is needed except the salt BEFORE cooking. After rice has cooked, add any additional seasoning like curry, oregano, basil, or parsley. Add butter just before serving. I usually make extra rice so I have some left-over for a different dish later in the week. This saves time. Just store the rice in an airtight container before adding the seasoning. Then you can use totally different seasonings and meat in the next meal. I may have chicken and rice with Italian seasoning one meal then, have an oriental rice dish with ginger, curry, soy sauce, Hoisin or black bean sauce later in the week. I only have to cook rice once, but I end up with two completely different meals.

Fried rice:

Making fried rice for an Asian meal is easy when you have leftover rice already cooked. Pour olive oil into nonstick skillet. Add fresh chopped onion (or previously sautéed onion stored in an airtight container). Then add garlic, red or green bell peppers, celery, and whatever you have on hand. Cole slaw mix (shredded cabbage and carrots) or any other veggie adds nice variety. Ginger, curry, or lemon pepper are good spices to sprinkle on while cooking. Soy sauce or Hoisin sauce can add flavor and a rich, brown color.

After veggies have sautéed, add the cooked rice. Stir and heat on medium. This is a great way to stretch the rice when you only have one serving and need to serve two people. Sometimes I bring home rice from a restaurant to use later as a side dish that I 'jazz up'. I'm not interested in eating plain rice. The 'doggie bag' rice can also be added when making soup. It takes a small amount to add texture to a soup.

Rice appetizer:

Rice can also be used as an appetizer. 1. Make a mound of rice on a salad plate, add a couple of fresh sautéed scallops or several cooked shrimp. Sprinkle corn, peas, bell peppers, etc. over the rice. 2. Make a small rice or risotto ball by adding a beaten egg and some cornmeal or raw grits. Add any seasoning you want – curry powder, parsley, etc. Pieces of fish or meat can also be added.

Heat olive oil in skillet. Cook until the rice ball is golden. This will look like a hush puppy.

Left-over rice in Gumbo:

Sauté chopped onion and garlic in oil. Add cooked sausage, chicken, shrimp, or a combination. While continuing to cook, add some frozen okra that has been rinsed and drained. Next add canned tomatoes that are chopped up and left-over rice. Season with fresh ground pepper, Creole seasoning like Tony's or a dash of cayenne or other hot sauce you have on hand. Add a sprinkle of sugar to all tomato sauces to bring out the flavors. Gumbo goes great with cornbread or French bread.

Couscous

Couscous is quick and easy. It looks and tastes exotic. I buy boxes that make multiple meals rather than the individual boxes that have seasonings added. The large boxes are much less expensive and allow the cook to add individual seasonings according to the meal being served.

Grits

Grits are also a great side that can be prepared according to directions on the box. I like to add grated cheese and/or sautéed garlic at the end of the cooking time.

Fresh Vegetables

Fresh Vegetables

Fresh vegetables are the best side any entrée could possibly have. Shopping to choose the freshest vegetables is of the utmost importance before cooking. Look for farmers' markets and grocery stores with a wide selection of produce. When vegetables are at their lowest price, they are usually in season and the freshest. This is the time to buy. Look for even color, texture, and shape. Mushy spots, brown spots, limp looking, or dull color tell the shopper 'keep looking, don't buy'.

Here are some of my favorite and easiest to prepare fresh vegetables. Always wash vegetables with cool running water before starting. Serve immediately after cooking. Vegetables are quick and easy and need to be cooked at the last minute so they are hot and not limp or soggy. Butter or cheese compliments any vegetable.

Asparagus

1. Cut off bottom 1-2 inches of stalk where it is thickest or whitest.
2. Leave stalks whole or cut in half or thirds.
3. Place in a glass pie plate, spread out in one layer.
4. Add a few tablespoons of water.
5. Cover with a dinner plate.
6. Cook 3-6 minutes in a microwave depending on the thickness of asparagus and how many you are cooking. Drain water.

7. I usually place the cooked asparagus on top of plain white rice then, smother rice and asparagus with butter. The rice is optional, butter is not!

Corn on the cob

1. Place about 1-2 inches water in the bottom of a large pot with a tight fitting lid. Turn stove heat to med. high.
2. Take off green husks and silky yellow parts covering the corn. Rinse in cool water.
3. Place corn in hot water. It should float. As soon as the water begins to boil, turn heat to very lowest setting. Make sure lid is in place.
4. Set timer for 10 minutes. Serve with butter.

Squash

1. Cut off both end pieces. Slice fairly thin or cube. Peeling is not necessary. Place in saucepan.
2. Cover with water. Add salt.
3. Bring to a boil, reduce heat to simmer. Use a lid.
4. Cook about 15 minutes or until squash is too tender to be picked up by a fork.
5. Drain in a colander. Add pepper and butter.
6. My favorite way to serve squash is with onions sautéed in butter. Cook chopped onions in lots of butter while squash is simmering. Combine onions with drained squash. Freshly ground pepper and salt perk up this side dish before serving.

Cauliflower or broccoli

1. Cut cauliflower or broccoli flowers from the main stalk. Cut larger pieces to bite size until all pieces are the same size. Cut away any brown spots. Only cut off the amount you need for each meal. Rewrap and return to refrigerator for future meal.
2. Place in a single layer in a pie plate. Add about 2 tablespoons water. Cover with a plate.
3. Cook in microwave 2-5 minutes depending on how large and how many pieces you have.
4. Drain in a colander.
5. Return to pie plate. Shape into individual servings. Cover with cheese-either grated or sliced. Microwave 30-60 seconds until melted.

Cole slaw

1. Buy prewashed shredded tri color cabbage in a plastic bag. This makes fresh Cole slaw so easy and fresh to mix just before serving.
2. In a mixing bowl, add very small amount of dressing and stir/toss to mix well. Bottled sauces can be found near the salad dressing or you can mix your own in a small bowl using mayonnaise or oil, some kind of vinegar (apple cider, raspberry, etc.) and some spices (salt, pepper, celery salt, lemon pepper, etc.)
3. Sometimes I like to add some drained canned fruit like pineapple or mandarin oranges after the slaw has been mixed together.

Frozen Foods

Frozen Foods

Frozen Pizza:

One of our favorite foods is pizza. I always keep several frozen pizzas in my freezer for a last minute meal or late night snack. Before cooking the pizza sometimes I lightly sprinkle it with dry instant grits to add flavor and texture. It looks like parmesan cheese. Next I find bits and pieces of fresh produce in my refrigerator like bell peppers, sautéed onions, mushrooms, chopped garlic in a jar, olive slices, etc. to sprinkle over the frozen pizza.

One of my most interesting and tasty items to add is a few slices of squash (any variety) sliced and quartered, cooked in the microwave about 30-40 sec. on a plate, then placed in a baggie with extra virgin olive oil, garlic, and Italian herbs and any other fresh produce like onions, mushrooms, or peppers. Toss in baggie until well coated with the oil. Place squash and friends on top of the pizza.

I first had pizza with squash as a topping when eating at an expensive Italian restaurant in Houston. I've added it to my frozen pizzas ever since.

Be creative in your pizza toppings. Spinach, feta cheese, and fresh tomatoes also make good toppings. For a seafood flavor, try canned clams or anchovies.

Now put the pizza in the oven while it's still preheating to toast the top ingredients. Watch carefully so you don't burn the toppings. As soon as you smell the toppings, turn oven dial to bake. Offer fresh grated parmesan cheese (not the kind you shake out of a can) after pizza is done.

To reheat pizza at a later date, place slices in a nonstick skillet on med/low heat to keep crust crisp or else heat in the oven. The microwave is not recommended since it makes the pizza soggy. Toaster ovens work great to reheat or to cook the pizza initially.

MEATBALLS:

Meatballs can be purchased frozen ready to use just like you would use hamburger meat, except it is already cooked. After the meatballs are heated according to package directions, they can be cut into 4-8 pieces each to be used in any dish like spaghetti, Mexican food, or Indian food. The bag can be twist tied for future use.

Sauces can be made to be added to the meatballs. The easiest white sauces are cream soups from a can such as cream of mushroom or cream of celery. Put soup in a bowl. Add some milk, half and half, sour cream, ranch dressing, or whatever liquid until it is the thickness you want. Add ground pepper or Italian spices to season.

You can add fresh sautéed onions, garlic or mushrooms give extra flavor. Heat the soup/sauce. Then add cooked meatballs.

Other Meatball suggestions:

At a party, serve with toothpicks. Offer a dipping sauce such as marinara or barbeque.

As a main dish, serve with a salad, bread and a vegetable.

Serve with a sauce on top of pasta or rice.

Fresh basil or chives on top of the finished dish or parsley on the side adds flavor and color.

Frozen vegetables:

A variety of frozen vegetables is essential to creating interesting meals.

I buy veggies in large plastic bags so they can easily be resealed with a bread tie since I only use a small amount in each meal.

All veggies are good in soups. Your soups will be unique every time with new combinations.

Frozen peas, carrots, broccoli, okra, corn, or vegetable medleys are great to add to leftover rice or pasta to stretch it for another meal and to add color.

I like to have bags of vegetable medleys available in my freezer such as Asian stir-fry vegetables or tricolor peppers with onions or winter vegetable mix or whatever is available at the grocery store that looks interesting and is versatile. I buy different combinations every grocery trip so we have lots of variety without repeating combinations for months. There are many good choices.

When making Chinese stir-fry, I like to add frozen vegetables along with fresh veggies (mushrooms, celery, onion, bell pepper) and/or canned veggies (bean sprouts, water chestnuts). Cashews, almonds, or peanuts are also a nice addition.

Frozen breads:

I like to repackage frozen rolls into small baggies when I first get home from the store. I select the number of rolls we eat in one meal to put in each baggie so there are no leftovers. At serving time, I usually defrost the bread in the microwave a few minutes before cooking.

Sometimes I buy fresh bakery bread. We eat the fresh bread the day I buy it then, I freeze meal size portions of the bread in baggies for the future. It's fun to have a variety of bread in the freezer to pull out at a moment's notice to complete a nice meal. Most microwaves have a defrost setting that makes using frozen bread even easier.

After defrosting, I place pats of salted real butter on the bread before placing bread under a broiler for just a couple of minutes to melt the butter and add a nice warm crust. Other heating variations are to top the sliced bakery bread with grated cheese or spread butter with garlic on the bread before warming in the toaster oven.

Some bakery breads taste better unheated served with an olive oil dipping sauce, other breads are better with butter. Let your taste buds decide which breads you like with olive oil and which you like with butter.

Mexican Style Meals

Mexican Style Meals

Quesadillas can be made with a variety of ingredients.

Basic recipe: flour tortillas + cheese

Side dish: beans or bean soup

Butter both sides of the tortilla before placing cheese and other ingredients on top of one side. Sometimes I make my quesadillas in the fold over style and sometimes I make them full size like a giant sandwich. Heat tortillas in a skillet or griddle on both sides until cheese melts and the tortilla is crispy. Cut the giant sandwich into 4 pieces. This is good for parties or when serving a group with lots of other food choices.

The typical Mexican quesadilla I grew up with just had Monterey jack and cheddar cheese inside with salt sprinkled on the outside after it was cooked.

Some of my favorite ingredients to add to the cheese are sautéed onions, celery, garlic, and spinach. Cut up chicken or bacon adds even more flavor. Limit the number of ingredients so the flavors retain their individuality. Too many flavors make a disaster. I like to use thinly grated cheese since it melts faster. Any cheese or cheese combinations will work as long as they blend with the added ingredients.

A side dish of beans goes well with quesadillas. This can be a bean soup, black beans, refried beans, pinto beans, etc.

Bean soup is easy to make. Add extra water to canned beans, add extra spices (chili powder, cumin, cayenne) plus maybe some onions, celery, or peppers. Chopped garden onion tops or fresh cilantro added to the top of the soup add color and flavor.

When turning the quesadillas, part of the filling sometimes falls out, especially if you put a lot of ingredients inside them. I like to put these crispy ingredients (that fell out when flipping the quesadilla) on top of my beans or bean soup. Also a dollop of sour cream goes well on top of the beans or a sprinkling of chopped green onions or fresh tomatoes. I sometimes offer bottled hot sauce with this meal especially if there aren't many fresh ingredients on the side.

Chile Rellenos

Last week the poblano peppers were on sale. They were a deep, rich green color with a firm texture. I couldn't resist the beautiful, fresh peppers. I love chili rellenos. On the day I cooked my peppers, I cut off the tops, saving the ring of pepper around the stem in a zip-lock bag for a later meal. I boiled the peppers whole while I sautéed some hamburger meat with onions, garlic, salt and pepper. For liquid I added a small can of tomato sauce and some mole sauce from a jar I found in my refrigerator. I also love mole sauce on left-over chicken. I also added a spoonful of sugar. Good cooks know to always add a little sugar when using tomato products. Next, I added some chopped pecans I had in my freezer, and some Cheddar cheese.

After mixing the liquid ingredients together, I added it to my meat mixture. Next I loaded the peppers with my meat and mole combination. I placed foil in a glass baking dish before adding the peppers. I put the stuffed peppers in the oven while it was on preheat, watching carefully so the peppers didn't burn, but just received a nice tan, then I turned the oven to bake.

Chile rellenos can also be stuffed with cheese only. A soft white Mexican cheese or grated blend of Cheddar, Colby, and Jack are a few ideas.

Mexican Meat Pie

A few days later I used some left-over meat mixture from my chile rellenos. I made some thick grits to use as the crust for a Mexican casserole. I sautéed more onions and left-over poblano pepper pieces in oil. Then I added the meat mixture with a touch of water to make it easy to heat in the skillet. I pressed the grits into an oiled pie pan, put meat mixture on top of that and then covered with cheese. I baked in preheat oven about 7-8 min, then on bake about 7-8 more min. I served it with sour cream on top. It was a tasty meal made in less than 30 min. My freezer always has homemade margaritas so that accompanied my Mexican pie.

Margaritas

Mix frozen limeade with water according to directions on can. Add an additional ½ - 1 can of tequila. Choose a fresh fruit like mango or watermelon. Peel and cube, then puree in food processor. Fruit juice also works – orange juice or fruit medley-about ½ can. Add fruit or fruit juice to lime/tequila mixture. Stir well. Pour into plastic container like a large margarine container with a lid. Freeze. Scoop out with an ice cream scooper when ready to serve in margarita glasses.

Avocados

Usually, avocados need to ripen before using so buy several days before you serve. Store the avocado in a dark place like inside a cabinet. Check it each day until it is soft, but not too mushy.

Sometimes the avocado is so perfect, I can't bear to mix it with anything else. When I first cut the avocado in half and I notice a beautiful color (no black spots), I remove the seed and serve the avocado in its shell with a small spoon. There are few flavors so intense and wonderful.

If the outer black shell peels off easily after removing the seed, and the fruit is firm with a nutty fragrance, the avocado is begging to be sliced into bite size pieces to be served fresh on a salad or as a side dish.

Guacamole

Fresh guacamole is quick, easy, and delicious! A small avocado will yield 2 servings. Cut around the widest part of the avocado with a sharp knife. It should easily open to reveal a huge seed. Discard the seed. Scoop out the soft green fruit with a spoon. Place in food processor with fresh onion, tomato, juice from a lime or lemon wedge, and salt. It only takes a little onion and tomato. If I don't have a fresh tomato I use a small spoon of a tomato based hot sauce or canned tomato. Blend until almost smooth. Taste. Add more salt if needed.

Spoon guacamole onto lettuce leaves to serve as a salad or use it on top of any Mexican entrée. Tortilla chips complement guacamole well.

Author Bio

Sandi Horton took her first cooking course at the age of ten with her Junior Girl Scout Troop. She has loved cooking ever since!

This cookbook was originally written as a wedding gift for her daughter. Requests for more books led to the creation of this book for public sale.

Today Sandi lives in Waco, Texas with her husband and a houseful of rescue dogs, mostly Boston terriers.

Every day is a culinary experience at the Horton House.

Made in the USA
Charleston, SC
11 September 2014